SAN FRANCISCO
Creation of a City

SAN FRANCISCO
Creation of a City

Tom Moulin and
Don DeNevi

Celestial Arts

MILLBRAE, CALIFORNIA

Celestial Arts
231 Adrian Road
Millbrae, California 94030

First printing, September, 1978

Made in the United States of America

Library of Congress Cataloging in Publication Data

Moulin, Tom, 1929-
    San Francisco, creation of a city.

    1. San Francisco—History—Pictorial works.   2. San Francisco—Description—Views.   I. DeNevi, Donald P., joint author.   II. Title.
F869.S343M68   779'.9'979461   78-54482
ISBN 0-89087-188-4
ISBN 0-89087-225-2 pbk.

    3   4   5   6   7   ——   85   84   83   82   81   80   79

interior design by Robert Hu

cover design by Abigail Johnston

You may order copies of any prints appearing in this book by writing to:

Moulin Studios
465 Green Street
San Francisco, CA 94133

This book is dedicated to the memory of my grandfather, Gabriel Moulin, a kind and gentle man who loved photography and made it an art.

— Tom Moulin

Simply for being, Martha Elin, this book is dedicated to you.

—Don DeNevi

Contents

Introduction

Much has been written about the history of San Francisco and many have photographed San Francisco, but none have captured the City over such a long period of time, and recorded it as artistically and as faithfully as the Moulin family. Nowhere is there a more beautiful historic record of San Francisco from the 1880s to the present than in their archives.

Gabriel Moulin was born in San Jose in 1872 of German and French parents. When he was twelve, the family moved to San Francisco and he left school to become a photographer, eventually finishing school at night. Soon after arriving in the City he went to work as an assistant with I. W. Taber, the City's leading photographer. The art of photography was still in its infancy, and most photographers were very secretive about their techniques. Gabriel was fortunate to have access to a studio where he could experiment and acquire the photographic secrets. During the day he earned his $12 per week salary, and by night learned developing and printing from the old timers in the lab.

By the 1894 Midwinter Fair in Golden Gate Park, young Gabriel had become an accomplished photographer. Approaching the turn of the century, San Francisco offered many visual attractions for the young photographer. The heavy camera equipment Moulin carried about the City did not dampen his enthusiasm, even while climbing the steep hills.

In 1898 Gabriel Moulin was asked to photograph at the Bohemian Club's encampment on the Russian River, and to make studies of the majestic redwood trees along the California coastline. Because of the contrast between the bright light and the black inky shadows that the trees cast, and the lack of modern photographic filters and equipment, photographing the redwoods was a challenge. Gabriel was able to master the situation using exposures of ten seconds to minutes and masterful techniques in developing the plates, for which he became known as the "Redwoods Photographer."

Shortly before 1900, Gabriel left Taber to join in forming R. J. Waters & Co. This association lasted until April 18, 1906—the day of the San Francisco earthquake and fire—when Gabriel pleaded with Waters to move all their precious negatives from their Ellis Street studio to save them from the advancing fires. Stubborn and unrealistic, Waters refused. Within hours, the entire collection, a priceless, irreplaceable visual history of San Francisco, was destroyed. That day, Gabriel began his career as an independent photographer, and many of his dramatic shots of the earthquake's aftermath established him as one of the City's most outstanding and creative photographers.

Gabriel Moulin was a very innovative and progressive photographer. Always a perfectionist, he sought to capture a perfectly composed photograph on his ground glass using his convertible lens (5" to 19"); never resorting to gimmickry or "arts" techniques, he strove to produce pure sharp images. Unlike other photographers, he did not create perfection in the photo lab by cropping the photo or embellishing the negative, but captured it with his camera, creating a perfection of balance, of framing, of vanishing point, and depth of field. This sense of balance and composition was the legacy he passed on to his sons, Irving and Raymond.

During the Panama-Pacific Exposition in 1915, Gabriel was the official photographer for the Palace of Fine Arts. He had been experimenting with the new Lumier color plates, and had refined the process so well that many of the prints he made of the original art on exhibition were sold at the Palace of Fine Arts.

When Irving and Raymond began to show an interest in photography, both boys took photographs at their school functions and developed them at their father's studio. Later, on the editorial staff of the *Daily Californian* at the University of California at Berkeley, Irving took most of the photographs for the school paper, while Raymond went to work in his father's studio.

Irving joined his father in business in 1923. Raymond, however, sought experience outside the family business, and in 1927 took a job in Los Angeles with the publishers of *Pictorial California* and traveled the state in a photographic and sales capacity. After returning to San Francisco toward the end of 1928, he worked at Californias Incorporated, an organization promoting travel in the still sparsely populated state, and briefly became a cruise photographer on a three-month trip to the Orient, South Pacific, and Australia. He returned in 1930, and shortly thereafter rejoined the family business.

Throughout the years, Moulin Studios has been in the forefront of innovative photography. Gabriel was always experimenting with photographic techniques—regulating the contrast of light and dark, varying exposures, trying new ways to develop negatives, and striving to capture the perfectly framed, perfectly balanced photograph. In 1933 Irving pioneered the use of photography for retail advertising in San Francisco and by the end of the year, every store in San Francisco that used illustrated advertising was a Moulin client for conversion of their photographs through the studio's line techniques. Raymond, meanwhile, had just designed an aerial camera for Moulin Studios and began making panoramic photographs of the City.

Moulin Studios was commissioned as the photographers for the construction of both the Golden Gate and the San Francisco-Oakland Bay Bridges. The mighty steel spans created breathtaking lines and artistry in their different phases of construction. Though Gabriel took many of the panoramic shots of both bridges, Raymond did most of the photography on the bridges themselves. Fearlessly climbing up towers and daring to negotiate catwalks, Raymond captured innumerable priceless photographs. One of his shots of the Bay Bridge was used on a postage stamp issued in 1938.

By the late 1930s, Moulin Studios was the major force on the West Coast in commercial and portrait photography. Although Gabriel worked out of his Kearny Street studio until his death, Moulin Studios purchased the building at 181 Second Street in 1937 and converted it into the finest photographic studio in the West. The studio was so big that the brothers once drove a Greyhound bus into it and set up a travel scene around it. Always in search of the unusual or unique photograph, the Moulins have done almost everything and gone to every extreme. They have ridden in cranes and helicopters, climbed to the tops of buildings and hills, and Raymond even rode the last steel beam as it was lifted up to the top of the 450 Sutter Building.

Moulin Studios has been involved in many varied projects. During World War II, they worked nights reproducing and enlarging maps and charts for the Department of Defense. Raymond traveled the United States taking travel pictures for Greyhound's yearly calendars. They have photographed every president of the Bank of America, and Irving took

the picture of A. P. Giannini that was later reproduced on a 25¢ postage
stamp. In 1950, they added a complete motion picture studio, and in 1936
had begun to create photomurals, then coming into vogue for interior
and exterior design. The studio was official photographer for the 1939
Golden Gate International Exposition.

Gabriel Moulin died in 1945, after more than sixty years as a
photographer. He had seen his beloved City through the most dynamic
phase of its growth, and had watched it grow from a boisterous
boomtown to a cosmopolitan metropolis. After Gabriel's death, Irving
and Raymond closed the Kearny Street studio, Gabriel's studio since he
had started in business for himself almost forty years before.

In 1957 Irving relinquished his share in the business, although he
continues to do some work for a few of his favorite clients. Raymond's
oldest son, Tom, began working in the family business in 1949, and in
1974 Raymond turned the business over to him. Now 73, Raymond has
retired to Hillsborough where he has a beautiful view of the San
Francisco skyline, and still picks up a camera whenever the studio needs
him. In 1974 Tom moved the studio from its Second Street location to
Green Street. Tom's son, Blake, the fourth generation of Moulin
photographers, joined the family business in 1975.

Gabriel taught his sons, who in turn have taught their sons, to look at
nature or a scene on the street and recognize in it the balance of elements
that create a beautiful photograph. Strength of light and shadow and the
dimensions created by it has always been a characteristic of Moulin
photography. The perfect photograph to a Moulin photographer is a
perfection of line, composition, and contrast of light and dark—a
photograph to make you stand back and say "ahh!"

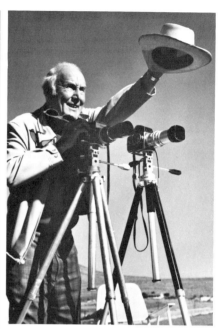

UPPER LEFT.   *Gabriel Moulin*
UPPER CENTER.   *Gabriel Moulin*
UPPER RIGHT.   *Raymond Moulin*
LOWER LEFT.   *Irving Moulin*
LOWER RIGHT.   *Tom Moulin*

The Early City

The San Francisco of the 1880s had undergone a striking change in appearance, culture, and character in the thirty-five years since the discovery of gold. The City was growing at a steady, even pace with its population approaching 300,000. The wild speculation and financial crashes of the previous three and a half decades had calmed and fortunes were no longer made or lost overnight. The once sleepy, sparsely populated pueblo of Yerba Buena was now known as San Francisco—the eighth largest city in the nation and center of trade on the West Coast. The maritime industry was opening up trade to Hawaii, the Orient, Australia, and Europe. The Ferry Building at the foot of Market Street was the point of embarkation for travelers, goods, and new settlers from all over the world.

The downtown business area was expanding and in the prosperous financial district new and larger buildings of stone, marble, and masonry were replacing the old fire-prone wooden structures. San Francisco was the banking capital of the West and in 1882 the San Francisco Stock Exchange was established. Market Street was now the main thoroughfare and the City's first "skyscraper," the ten-story *Chronicle* building, was completed.

Throughout the City major building projects were under way. A new City Hall and Hall of Records were being erected; the lavish Palace Hotel was completed and offered some of the most luxurious accommodations anywhere; and in the western part of the City a magnificent park of over 1,000 acres, Golden Gate Park, was being created on top of the sand dunes. The feeling of San Francisco—of grandness, of challenge, of opportunity—prevailed.

1

Due to a stable prosperity, increasing trade, and dreams of getting rich quick, San Francisco was becoming congested, and the residential areas began expanding. The invention of the cable car brought easy access to steep hilltops and enabled wealthy residents to build mansions that offered spectacular views of the City and the Bay. Nob Hill and Russian Hill replaced South Park and Rincon Hill as the most fashionable places to live in the City. With the extension and improvement of streetcar service to Golden Gate Park and out to the beach, families were now able to live farther from the center of the City, and the "wastelands" and sand dunes of outlying districts that had previously been considered uninhabitable slowly began developing into residential areas.

With the completion of the railroad, thousands upon thousands of Chinese had now settled into a twelve-square-block area in the heart of the City. The Chinese, brought over by the "Big Four" financial barons to provide cheap labor, now found themselves unemployed and resettled in a small, densely populated area.

The atmosphere was vibrant, it was high spirited, it was reckless; people were positive, and open; energy of every kind abounded. San Franciscans took pride in their City and had a love for what had been, and was being, created. What had been a vast, largely unpopulated area of sand dunes and marshes sixty years earlier now astonished even its own residents with its rapid growth. San Francisco flourished—until April 18, 1906.

Looking from Russian Hill toward the wharves. (1880s)

4

LEFT. *The Central Terminal Building, built in 1877. (about 1886)*

ABOVE. *Alcatraz Island. (1880s)*

RIGHT. *Mission Dolores, San Francisco's second permanent structure, established 1776, after the garrison at the Presidio that same year. In the adjoining graveyard are buried many of the City's earliest explorers and pioneers.*

ABOVE.   *The City Transfer Company on Eddy Street. (about 1890)*

CENTER.   *Union Square, 1880s. The Hopkins and Stanford mansions on Nob Hill in the distance.*

RIGHT.   *The Merchant's Exchange, center, in the 400 block of California Street. Nob Hill in the distance. (1880s)*

6

ABOVE. *Looking down Market Street from the Ferry Building. Right center is the unfinished Merchant's Exchange on California Street. Up California Street is the unfinished Fairmont Hotel on Nob Hill.*

RIGHT. *Union Square, 1903. The Dewey monument in the center of the square is being erected, and across the street the foundation for the Saint Francis Hotel is being laid.*

9

LEFT. *Market Street at Montgomery, the Crocker Building. The clock tower of the* Chronicle *Building is beyond.*

RIGHT. *One block down Market Street, looking from Third Street across Market to Kearny. Near right is the Hearst Building, home of the San Francisco* Examiner. *Across the street is the de Young, or* Chronicle *Building. (1890s)*

ABOVE.   *Looking up Mason Street toward Nob Hill, where the Fairmont Hotel is still unfinished. The tall building near right is the Saint Francis Hotel on Union Square, now complete. (1904)*

RIGHT.   *Looking north from Rincon Hill. Nob Hill is on the left, with Russian Hill beyond it. In the center is the new Merchant's Exchange building, and the Selby shot tower is in the right foreground. Telegraph Hill is on the right. (about 1902)*

12

13

14

LEFT.   *The Hall of Justice, Portsmouth Square.*

ABOVE.   *Robert Louis Stevenson monument in Portsmouth Square in front of the Hall of Justice. Erected 1897.*

ABOVE RIGHT.   *City Hall. The Pioneer monument in front was given to San Francisco in 1894 by James Lick. (about 1901)*

RIGHT.   *The Hall of Records on Leavenworth and McAllister Streets. (about 1900)*

15

ABOVE.　*The Cliff House overlooking Seal Rock and the Pacific Ocean. The first in the series of Cliff Houses to occupy the site, it was built in 1864 and burned in 1894. On the bluff above is Sutro Heights, home of Adolph Sutro, and on the beach to the right is a popular dance hall. (late 1880s)*

RIGHT.　*The second Cliff House, built by Adolph Sutro, was sometimes referred to as "Sutro's gingerbread palace." This view from Sutro Heights was taken in 1907, just before this one also went up in flames.*

ABOVE. *The Mark Hopkins (left) and Leland Stanford mansions on Nob Hill.*

RIGHT. *California Street, Nob Hill. The Flood (near right), Huntington, and Crocker mansions.*

ABOVE. *The corner of Geary, Kearny, and Market Streets.*
(March 31, 1906)

RIGHT. *Pine Street west of Dupont (now Grant Avenue).*
(1905)

20

The City Devastated

At 5:13 on the morning of April 18, 1906, San Francisco shuddered under a violent earthquake. Chimneys toppled into the streets, entire buildings were shaken down, and streets were littered with bricks, debris, and twisted streetcar tracks. The majority of buildings withstood the quake well; those that didn't were of poor construction or were built on filled land. Though the City was badly shaken, no one yet realized what the extent of the damage would eventually be.

Fires caused by overturned wooden stoves and broken gas mains soon began to break out, and the wooden houses that comprised most of the City began to catch fire. Most of the water mains, desperately needed to combat the spreading fires, had been broken by the temblor. Soon the water supply ran out and firefighters were powerless to stop the advancing flames. By the late afternoon of April 18, the area south of Market Street was in cinders, and the flames were spreading along the waterfront and across Market to the business district. Dynamite was even used to try to halt the advance of the searing flames. The seriousness of the disaster was becoming apparent.

By the time the colossal fire was brought under control three days later, over 28,000 buildings covering an area of four and a half square miles had been gutted or destroyed. Most of the business and industrial sections had been lost. The heart of San Francisco, from south of Market to Nob Hill, from the waterfront to Van Ness Avenue, lay in charred ruins. Nearly a quarter of a million people were homeless, and transportation and utilities were virtually nonexistent.

Mayor Eugene Schmitz issued a dusk-to-dawn curfew and called out federal troops from the Presidio to help curb looting and crime.

Distribution centers to provide food, clothing, blankets, and other necessities were set up, and public parks and squares were soon covered with tents or improvised shacks. Until broken chimneys, water and gas mains could be inspected and repaired, all cooking had to be done outdoors. Standing in line for rations was an experience shared by everyone, regardless of social or financial status before the quake.

As soon as the fires died down, San Franciscans threw themselves wholeheartedly into the task of rebuilding their beloved City. Downtown, hundreds of workers and volunteers worked around the clock clearing away the rubble and wreckage. Temporary streetcar tracks were laid and thousands of units of temporary housing were built; businesses salvaged what they could and reopened in residences that had been beyond the reach of the flames while their offices downtown were being rebuilt.

Three years after the earthquake and fire had devastated the City, 20,500 of the buildings destroyed had been rebuilt. Because of the recent disaster, most of the new structures were built to be earthquake-proof, and were superior to the old in design, quality, and materials used. San Franciscans were proving to the world that with their indomitable spirit, they could even rebuild an entire city.

A panoramic view of the Embarcadero from Nob Hill. On the right is Grace Church on California Street. The Ferry Building is visible in the distance. Offshore is Yerba Buena Island.

24

LOWER LEFT. *A door frame in the financial district.*

LOWER RIGHT. *The Hall of Justice, Portsmouth Square. Tents and cooking facilities set up in the Square.*

RIGHT. *Fulton Street.*

LEFT. *Union Street, west of Steiner.*

UPPER RIGHT. *Howard Street between 17th and 18th Streets.*

LOWER RIGHT. *Standing in the ration line at Golden Gate Park.*

ABOVE. *Clearing away the wreckage on Mission Street, the domes of City Hall and the Hall of Records in the background.*

LEFT. *Temporary telephone service.*

RIGHT. *Produce and supplies were sold in the streets until shops could be rebuilt.*

FAR LEFT. *The view down Market Street from the top of the Ferry Building. Temporary streetcar tracks are being laid and rubble cleared away.*

LEFT. *The same view one year after the earthquake and fire.*

ABOVE. *Looking down Market Street toward the Ferry Building one year after the quake. Offshore is Yerba Buena Island.*

RIGHT. *The white marble portico was all that remained of the Towne residence on Nob Hill. Since removed to Golden Gate Park, the portico now stands beside a small lake, and is appropriately referred to as the "Portals of the Past." Beyond Nob Hill, the City is being rebuilt as the skyline rises one year after the disaster.*

San Francisco Hosts the World

In early 1906 a bill was pending before Congress that would have named San Francisco the city to host a world's fair commemorating the completion of the Panama Canal. The earthquake caused those plans to be laid aside as San Franciscans devoted their energy and attention to rebuilding their City. In 1907, with the reconstruction well under way, San Francisco was again anxious to host the Exposition and show itself, newly rebuilt, to the world.

The site chosen for the Panama-Pacific Exposition was the waterfront area on San Francisco's northern shore, inside the Golden Gate. The work of building a sea wall and filling in 184 acres of shallows to transform the marshy, undeveloped tidelands into land that could be built upon began in 1911.

When the Exposition opened on February 20, 1915, the area had been transformed into a fairyland of architecture and light. Ten exhibition palaces opened onto a series of interlinked courtyards, forming the central part of the exposition. In the center of this, the Tower of Jewels rose majestically. A small harbor at the foot of the site allowed ferry transportation directly to the area and provided an arena for water pageants. The landscaping of the grounds was supervised by John McLaren, superintendent of Golden Gate Park, whose concept of landscape gardening as an art was beautifully exemplified by the magnificent gardens and tree-lined walks.

The Exposition closed eleven months later on December 4, 1915. Almost 19 million people from around the world had visited the spectacular Exposition, and San Francisco had won the admiration of the world.

FAR LEFT. *The Exposition site before the work of filling in the land, building a harbor, and constructing the Exposition began.*

ABOVE. *The opening ceremonies.*

LEFT. *The speakers' podium and spectators' gallery at the opening ceremonies.*

38

LEFT. *The Palace of Fine Arts, majestic and melancholy, was the Exposition's most popular and cherished sight. The Palace was designed by Bernard Maybeck, who sought to produce an effect of "sadness modified by the feeling that beauty has a soothing influence."*

ABOVE. *The Moulin family at the Exposition. Sons Raymond and Irving are on each side in the front.*

RIGHT. *The landscape gardening, directed by John McLaren, in front of the columns of the Palace of Fine Arts.*

ABOVE. *The amusement area, or "The Zone."*

NEAR RIGHT. *The Chinese exhibit.*

FAR RIGHT. *The Palace of Horticulture.*

42

LEFT. *The Tower of Jewels, described as an "architectural wedding cake shimmering with gems of purest glass," dominated the center of the Exposition.*

ABOVE. *The Palace of Education.*

ABOVE RIGHT. *The pool in the central courtyard.*

OVERLEAF. *The Exposition grounds.*

Edith Woodman Burrough's "Fountain of Youth."

46

The Magic Metropolis

With the close of the Panama-Pacific Exposition in 1915, San Francisco continued its rapid growth. The burst of coordinated city planning inspired by the Exposition was drawing to an end as the new Civic Center complex neared completion. The nation was now in the middle of World War I, and San Francisco, with the largest natural harbor on the West Coast, had much of its shipping industry converted to wartime use. The waterfront, shipyards, and related industries were built up or improved, and the population swelled with the influx of military personnel and workers in the war industry.

In the downtown area, the increasing size and number of hotels, restaurants, and shops was phenomenal. Year after year, the skyline that residents and tourists alike found so enchanting was rising higher and higher. Chinatown, North Beach, and other neighborhoods were becoming increasingly attractive and offered many exotic foods and imported goods. Outlying areas that had only begun to be settled were now mushrooming into populous residential districts with row after row of new houses being laid out.

Though San Franciscans have often been accused of being too individualistic and too rowdy, they have always had a reverence for culture. Since the mid 1800s, San Francisco has had both theater and musical troupes, and when the War Memorial Opera House was completed in the 'thirties, the symphony and opera both found permanent homes. Theaters proliferated around Union Squre, and in other parts of San Francisco small playhouses and theater groups sprang up. The cultural heritage of the City is evident not only in its numerous art galleries, but also in places such as restaurants, coffeehouses, Aquatic Park, Coit Tower, and the colorful street artists and fairs.

San Franciscans work hard and play hard. Nowhere was this more evident than at the beach, where in the 1920s several spectacular projects were completed. The Great Highway and Esplanade ran along the beach. You could stroll along this three-mile stretch and choose from a number of attractions—swimming at Sutro Baths or Fleishhacker Pool, visiting the animals at the Fleishhacker Zoo, entertainment at the huge amusement park, Playland-at-the-Beach, or wining and dining at the famous Cliff House overlooking the waters of the Pacific. On a Sunday afternoon thousands of San Franciscans in pursuit of leisure picnicked on the beach or strolled along the Esplanade taking in the sea breezes, the sun, and in the evening, the glorious Pacific sunset.

First and Market and Bush Streets, about 1915. In front is the Mechanics monument, erected in 1894.

The Ferry Building at the foot of Market Street. Beyond are Yerba Buena Island and the hills of Oakland and Berkeley across the Bay.

Looking southwest on Market Street, Twin Peaks in the distance.

FAR LEFT. *The Wells Fargo-Nevada National Bank on Market and Montgomery, tower of the Hobart Building on Market Street behind it. (about 1910)*

CENTER. *Looking north on Second Street to Market at the Hobart Building designed by Lewis P. Hobart, one of the City's leading architects.*

ABOVE. *The clock tower of the Ferry Building rises at the foot of Market Street. On the left, California Street runs into Market. When streets were laid out, Market was laid parallel to the old mission road (Mission Street), northeast to southwest. Streets were later planned to run north-south and east-west.*

LEFT. *Market Street, about 1916.*

RIGHT. *One of the many flower stands in the downtown area. This one is on Grant Avenue.*

54

FAR LEFT.   *Market and Powell Streets, the end of the line for the Powell Street cable car. On the right corner is the Flood Building, and across the street is the Bank of Italy, later the Bank of America. Nob Hill is in the background. (1920s)*

LEFT.   *Market near Fifth Street. (1920s)*

FAR LEFT.   *The Saint Francis Hotel on Union Square. (1920s)*

ABOVE LEFT.   *Union Square by Christmas light.*

ABOVE RIGHT   *Looking from the corner of Union Square at the City of Paris, one of the City's most elegant places to shop.*

RIGHT   *City of Paris window.*

RIGHT.   *The Orpheum Theater on Market Street opened in 1926 as a vaudeville theater, and continues to stage plays of all kinds.*

LOWER LEFT.   *The Bohemian Club, Taylor and Post, 1920s. This structure was torn down in 1930 in order to build the new club.*

LOWER RIGHT.   *Shreve's on Post Street and Grant Avenue has been offering San Franciscans the finest in unique jewelry and gifts since the Shreve brothers first founded it in San Francisco in 1852.*

ABOVE LEFT.   *The Sir Francis Drake Hotel on Powell and Sutter Streets. (1928)*

ABOVE RIGHT.   *The Clift Hotel on Geary Street.*

FAR LEFT.   *The new City Hall and Civic Center complex. The Exposition Auditorium is on the left of the square, and the library near right. The old City Hall stood in back of the Pioneer monument on the corner.*

LEFT.   *San Francisco's main Public Library.*

BELOW.   *One of the many reading rooms.*

FAR LEFT. *Looking at the Van Ness Avenue entrance to City Hall; the War Memorial Opera House on the right, and the Veterans Building on the left.*

ABOVE LEFT. *Van Ness Avenue in front of the Opera House and Veterans Building.*

LEFT. *Opening night at the opera.*

FAR LEFT. *Portsmouth Square, where John B. Montgomery, captain of the* U. S. S. Portsmouth, *first raised the American flag over San Francisco.*

ABOVE. *The Hall of Justice, Portsmouth Square. (1920s)*

LEFT. *Robert Louis Stevenson monument in Portsmouth Square. Chinatown is in the background.*

LEFT. *Chinatown. (early 1900s)*

ABOVE. *Grant Avenue.*

ABOVE RIGHT. *Chinatown. (early 1900s)*

LEFT. *The Grant Avenue entrance to Chinatown.*
ABOVE. *Grant Avenue.*
RIGHT. *The Chinese New Year Parade, 1939.*

The Liverpool, London, & Globe Insurance Building
on Leidesdorff and California Streets, built in 1909.
The clock in front was built by the watchmaker to the Queen
in 1876 and was brought around the Horn to San Francisco.
Across the street is the San Francisco National Bank. (about
1917)

Detail of San Francisco National Bank. Organized in 1897,
it was absorbed by the Bank of California in 1920.

RIGHT. *Looking up California Street to Nob Hill. On the right*
side of the street you can see the clock in front of the
Liverpool, London, & Globe Insurance Building. On the right
corner is the Bank of California.

LEFT. *The Standard Oil Building on Bush and Sansome Streets. (1920s)*

ABOVE. *The Bank of America Building on California and Montgomery Streets. (1920s)*

RIGHT. *The Bank of California on Sansome and California Streets. Organized in 1867 on this site, the original building was torn down shortly before the earthquake.*

LEFT. *Looking northeast on Market Street, the financial district clustered on the left. (late 1930s)*

ABOVE. *The financial district from Telegraph Hill.*

FAR RIGHT. *Montgomery Street, the "Wall Street of the West." (1920s)*

LEFT. *The Stock Exchange on Pine Street, the Russ Building lighted beyond. Formerly the United States Subtreasury Building, it was extensively remodeled in 1928 when it became the Stock Exchange. Formerly the site of James Fair's home.*

ABOVE. *The floor of the Pacific Coast Stock Exchange when it was located on Montgomery Street. (1927)*

LEFT.   *The buildings of the financial district dominate the evening skyline. (1930s)*

UPPER RIGHT.   *The distinctive roof of the 111 Sutter Building (the Hunter Dulin Building), formerly the site of the Lick House, owned by James Lick. In the background on Market Street are the Hobart Building and the Call Building. Beyond is the Telephone Building (flag on top), south of Market Street.*

LOWER RIGHT.   *The Telephone Building from the area south of Market Street. (1920s)*

ABOVE.   *The Chronicle moved to this, its present site, at Fifth and Mission, in 1924.*

RIGHT.   *Old Seals Stadium, Sixteenth and Bryant Streets.*

ABOVE LEFT.   *The luxurious Palace Hotel at Market and New Montgomery Streets opened in 1875. Gutted by fire after the earthquake, it was rebuilt on the same lavish scale.*

ABOVE.   *The Court of the Sun, carriage entrance to the Palace Hotel.*

RIGHT.   *The carriage entrance is now the Garden Court restaurant. The table centerpiece is a replica of the Tower of the Sun at the Golden Gate Exposition. (1939)*

LEFT.   The Ferry Building at the foot of
Market Street was for decades the point of
embarkation for travelers and ferry
passengers. This, the second Ferry Building,
replaced the Central Terminal Building. It
was completed in 1903, its clock tower
modeled after the Giralda Tower in Seville,
Spain. Yerba Buena Island is offshore.
(1930s)

UPPER RIGHT.   Cars line up to drive onto the
transbay ferries. (1920s)

RIGHT.   The Embarcadero and downtown
San Francisco. The Ferry Building is on the
right. (late 1920s)

The waterfront and Bay from Telegraph Hill.

The Hunter's Point drydocks.

Fisherman's Wharf.

LEFT.   *Domingo Ghirardelli moved his chocolate and spice factory to North Point Street in 1897, taking over the brick buildings abandoned by Columbia Woolen Mills.*

ABOVE.   *Aquatic Park, Telegraph Hill beyond. On the hill directly behind the Maritime Museum, right, is the Ghirardelli chocolate factory. The row of brick buildings on the left is the Del Monte cannery. (1930s)*

LEFT. *The San Francisco yacht harbor in the Marina district.*   ABOVE. *The Scott Street pier, with the Golden Gate Yacht Club in the background.*

Telegraph Hill, about 1915.

Coit Tower, the gift of Lily Hitchcock Coit, stands as a monument to the volunteer firefighters of the 1850s and 1860s.

LEFT. *Lombard Street, the "crookedest street in the world" on Russian Hill.*

UPPER LEFT. *The Fairmont and Mark Hopkins Hotels on Nob Hill. Begun in 1902, the Fairmont (left) was nearly complete at the time of the earthquake. Its interior gutted by fire, it was restored and opened in 1907. The Mark Hopkins, built in 1926, occupies the site of the former Mark Hopkins residence.*

LOWER LEFT.   *Once the residence of James Flood, this Nob Hill brownstone was restored after the earthquake and fire, and now houses the prestigious Pacific Union Club.*

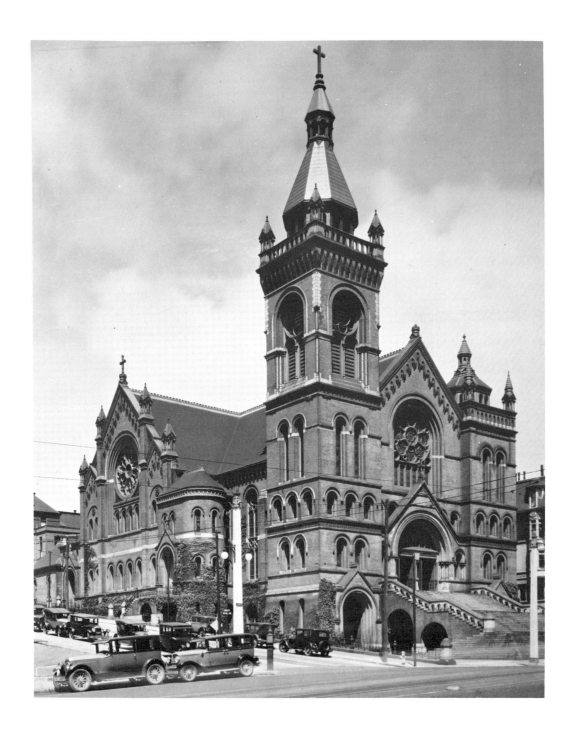

LEFT. *Saint Mary's Church on Van Ness Avenue.*

RIGHT. *The Church of Saints Peter and Paul on Filbert Street.*

LEFT. *Old Saint Mary's Church on Grant Avenue and California Street. Built in the 1850s, it survived the great earthquake.*

RIGHT. *Mission Dolores on Dolores Street was built in 1776.*

LEFT. *The old band shell in Golden Gate Park. 1880s.*

BELOW. *The children's playground in Golden Gate Park. (1880s)*

RIGHT. *The conservatory, built in 1877, was a gift to the City from the Crocker family.*

Stow Lake, Golden Gate Park.

The Japanese Tea Garden is the only attraction created for the 1894 Midwinter Fair that remains today.

ABOVE. *The Portals of the Past.*

NEAR RIGHT. *Sheep once roamed the Park's grassy expanses.*

FAR RIGHT. *Murphy's windmill, built in 1907, helps pump water for the Park's irrigation system.*

FAR LEFT.   *The de Young Museum, overlooking the music concourse and bandshell.*

LEFT.   *The Fine Arts Building, the first museum in Golden Gate Park, was built for the 1894 Midwinter Fair. Replaced by the de Young Museum, the two sphinxes, the bronze lion, and the sun dial are all that remain today of the Fine Arts Building.*

BELOW.   *The drive in front of the conservatory. (1920s)*

ABOVE. *The Palace of Fine Arts, designed by Bernard Maybeck, is the only structure that remains from the 1915 Panama-Pacific Exposition.*

UPPER RIGHT. *The Palace of the Legion of Honor in Lincoln*

Park is a memorial to the Californians who died in the first World War. In its courtyard is one of the five original casts of Rodin's The Thinker.

LOWER RIGHT. *The garden at the Palace of the Legion of Honor.*

113

FAR LEFT. *An aerial view of Sutro Baths and the Cliff House on the Great Highway.*

UPPER LEFT. *Sutro Baths, built in 1896 by Adolph Sutro, was the world's largest indoor pool, and housed six pools of varying temperatures and depths.*

LOWER LEFT. *Fleishhacker Pool, the world's largest outdoor pool, is 1,000 feet long and 150 feet wide and is filled with sea water pumped from the nearby Pacific Ocean.*

116

FAR LEFT. *Stern Grove, a large park on Sloat Boulevard and Nineteenth Avenue, holds various celebrations throughout the year and offers free concerts on summer Sunday afternoons.*

UPPER LEFT. *The Cliff House on the Great Highway.*

LOWER LEFT. *The view from Sutro Heights along the Great Highway. Playland-at-the-Beach is on the left. Beyond Playland is the western end of Golden Gate Park, and the undeveloped sand dunes of what is now the residential Sunset district.*

Two Bridges and a Celebration

Over the years, San Francisco and the surrounding Bay area had grown into a large, metropolitan region. Every day thousands commuted into the City by ferry or train. As the population and the use of automobiles increased, it became evident that the ferries would not be able to handle the traffic indefinitely. As early as the 1850s, bridges from San Francisco to the East Bay and to Marin County had been proposed—sometimes fancifully, sometimes seriously—and now in the 1930s, the dreams were to become reality. And in true San Francisco style, a world's fair was planned to celebrate the bridge completions.

Opposition to the bridges came from conservationists, the ferries, railroads, timber interests, and those who feared bridges would spoil the natural beauty of San Francisco Bay; some skeptics doubted they could be built at all. In January of 1933, construction of the bridge from San Francisco across the Golden Gate to Marin County, the longest suspension bridge in the world was begun.

Six months later, in July 1933, work began on the San Francisco-Oakland Bay Bridge. The Bay Bridge stretched from San Francisco's eastern shore through the Yerba Buena Island tunnel to Oakland. Hailed as the "world's longest over-water span," the Bay Bridge opened on November 12, 1936, and San Francisco businesses and residents held a three-day jubilee to celebrate its opening. Five months later, on May 27, 1937, the Golden Gate Bridge opened, and San Francisco was linked with the northern and eastern edges of the Bay.

To celebrate the completion of the bridges, San Francisco held a world's fair. The site for the exposition was created out of the shoals off Yerba Buena Island. Boundaries were marked off, and the land filled, in part, with dredgings from the Bay Bridge foundations and rock blasted from Yerba Buena Island during the construction of the tunnel. Upon the newly created island, Treasure Island, rose the towers and pavilions of the Golden Gate International Exposition. Subtitled "A Pageant of the Pacific," the Exposition celebrated not only the completion of the bridges, but also the hope of an era of increasingly friendly relations between nations of the Pacific.

Described as an attempt to "strike a golden medium between pageantry and structural beauty," the finished exposition was an island wonderland surrounded by the sparkling waters of San Francisco Bay. Ralph Stackpole's huge statue "Pacifica" dominated the central courtyard, and many other Bay area sculptors, architects, and mural painters contributed to the art and architecture. John McLaren supervised the landscape gardening.

The Exposition was open for two seasons, the first from February to the end of October, 1939, and the second from May to September, 1940, and was visited by over 17 million people. As World War II approached, the opulent grounds of the Exposition gave way to the military, as the United States Navy took over the site.

The Golden Gate Bridge

LEFT.   *The towers of the Golden Gate Bridge in the foreground, and the towers of the San Francisco-Oakland Bay Bridge in the background.*

ABOVE   *The beginning of the bridge, photographed from Lincoln Park.*

ABOVE. *The north tower of the Golden Gate Bridge. The spans of the Bay Bridge are beyond.*

RIGHT. *Looking down from the top of the San Francisco tower of the Golden Gate Bridge.*

122

LEFT. *The view from the north tower across the catwalks to San Francisco.*

BELOW. *Working on the massive steel beams. At the bottom is the safety net.*

LEFT.   *From Lincoln Park golf course, the bridge is in the final stages of construction.*

BELOW LEFT.   *Standing under the San Francisco approach roadway to the bridge, construction nearly completed.*

BELOW RIGHT.   *The roadway into San Francisco, the expanses of the Presidio beyond.*

LOWER LEFT: *Looking from the San Francisco shore to Marin, the arch at the San Francisco terminus of the bridge was specially constructed to save Fort Winfield Scott, the historic fort that has guarded the entrance to the bay since 1861.*

RIGHT: *Night view, nearing completion.*

Opening day, May 26, 1937.

132

The Bay Bridge

LEFT.   *Yerba Buena Island before the bridge was begun.*

ABOVE LEFT.   *The San Francisco tower of the Bay Bridge.*

ABOVE RIGHT.   *The ferries on their way from the East Bay to San Francisco. Beyond are the hills of San Francisco— Mount Davidson with its cross atop, Twin Peaks, and Mount Sutro.*

138

The tunnel through Yerba Buena Island.

The San Francisco terminus of the bridge.

The roadway, newly completed.

ABOVE.   *The opening of the bridge, November 12, 1936.*   RIGHT.   *The bridges at dusk.*

144

The Exposition

ABOVE.   *Gabriel Moulin's Exposition ticket book.*

LEFT.   *Ground-breaking ceremonies for the Exposition, May 21, 1937.*

LEFT.   *The Exposition under construction.*

ABOVE.   *The Tower of the Sun under construction.*

RIGHT.   *The Exposition grounds.*

150

ABOVE. *The amusement section at the Exposition, the "Gayway."*

RIGHT. *The Elephant Gate, the main entrance to the Exposition.*

ABOVE. *The Court of Pacifica, the statue "Pacifica" by Ralph Stackpole at the head of the Court. At the opposite end of this court is the Court of the Sun.*

RIGHT. *"Pacifica" and fountain in the Court of Pacifica.*

154

LEFT. *The Court of the Sun by night.*

ABOVE. *The Sun Tower rises majestically over the Court of the Sun, the waterfall of the Court of Pacifica in the foreground.*

157

The City

Sailboats and ferry boats, hilltops and valleys, magnificent hotels and intimate sidewalk cafes, lakes and beaches, parks and museums, breathtaking vistas and colorful streets, cable cars and rapid transit, and of course, the bridges—it is all San Francisco. Over the years, San Francisco has been called many things—the Gold Rush City, the Gateway to the Pacific, the Financial Capital of the West, Baghdad by the Bay, the City of Dreams, the City of Love. Strangely, it has been, and still is, all of these things. It is this blend of old and new that gives San Francisco its aura of timelessness. A photographer's paradise and a poet's dream.

The City is always in the process of creation. New buildings replace the old and add their rooftops to the picturesque skyline. Pre-earthquake buildings and houses stand alongside their modern counterparts; street names recall the City's early pioneers and settlers; and civic projects like Union Square and Golden Gate Park, begun long ago, still give pleasure and pause today. New construction projects and transportation systems, old Victorian houses continually being renovated, and neighborhoods adding their character and color to an atmosphere charged with energy and individuality.

Beautiful old buildings like the Ghirardelli chocolate factory and the Del Monte cannery have been saved from demolition and converted into charming shops, boutiques, and restaurants. The Cliff House still looks out on Seal Rock and the waters of the Pacific, but its former neighbors, the Sutro Baths, Playland-at-the-Beach, and Fleishhacker Pool, are no more. Ferry boats again chug the Bay waters, the views from the hills are still awe inspiring, and fingers of fog still creep in in the late afternoons just as they have for thousands of years. The City is timeless, indestructible, seemingly immortal.

It is said that San Francisco will never grow old, that the City will go on forever—and well it might. For when you look at the City as dusk approaches and the lights begin to flicker on, it is sometimes hard to distinguish between where the lights on the hills leave off and the stars begin.

LEFT. *The Hobart Building on Market Street, left, and the 111 Sutter Building, center, on Sutter and Montgomery Streets. Up Sutter Street is the Sir Francis Drake Hotel. (1950s)*

CENTER. *Maiden Lane. (1950s)*

RIGHT. *The corner of Powell and Market Streets, the turnaround for the Powell Street cable car. (1950s)*

160

FAR LEFT. *The eastern edge of Golden Gate Park and its Panhandle extension. The twin-spired Saint Ignatius Church on Fulton is on the right, Lone Mountain College is on the hill behind it. Beyond is San Francisco Bay and the hills of Marin.*

NEAR LEFT. *Grace Cathederal on Nob Hill.*

BELOW. *The Marina district and Aquatic Park with its circular sea wall. Alcatraz is in the foreground.*

164

LEFT.   *An aerial view of Nob Hill (foreground), downtown, the waterfront, and the Bay Bridge.*

ABOVE LEFT.   *The California Street cable cars as they pass through part of Chinatown on their way down to Market Street and up to Nob Hill. On the left, behind the upturned roof of a Chinese pagoda, is the clock tower of Old Saint Mary's Church, built in the 1850s. The Bay Bridge is beyond.*

ABOVE RIGHT.   *A playground in the Panhandle.*

ABOVE. *Ghirardelli Square today—shops and restaurants, and still making a little chocolate.*

LEFT. *The Cannery. (1978)*

RIGHT. *Fisherman's Wharf. (1978)*

166

The Saint Francis Hotel on Union Square, its new addition, the Saint Francis Tower, rising behind it. In the early forties, Union Square was dug up and a garage built underneath. The square was restored and is still a haven for those resting, feeding pigeons, or just absorbing the sun and the sights. (1974)

168

*The Justin Herman Plaza at the end of Market Street,
where artists sell their wares. Across the street is the clock
tower of the Ferry Building. (1978)*

FAR LEFT. *Saint Mary's Cathedral on Cathedral Hill was completed in 1970. It replaced Saint Mary's Church on Van Ness Avenue and O'Farrell Street, which burned in 1962.*

LEFT. *The Crown Zellerbach Building and the round Wells Fargo Bank on Market Street.*

ABOVE. *The Crown Zellerbach Building towers above the Mechanics monument.*

The San Francisco skyline today.

Index